Five in the Family

by DOROTHY BARUCH *and* ELIZABETH MONTGOMERY

WILLIAM S. GRAY, *Reading Director*

Illustrated by Miriam Story Hurford

HEALTH AND PERSONAL DEVELOPMENT SERIES

CURRICULUM FOUNDATION PROGRAM

Scott, Foresman and Company

CHICAGO ATLANTA DALLAS NEW YORK

A Birthday in the Family

Jack and the New Neighbors

Sue and Her Friends

Fun with Tommy

A Busy Mother and Father

Jack's Birthday Again

A Birthday in the Family

Happy Birthday

It was Jack's birthday, and the family was looking at some pictures of him.

"Oh!" laughed Jack. "Here I was on my very first birthday."

"This is how you looked at three," Father said. "And here you are at five."

"I like last year's picture," said Sue. "Tommy and I were in it, too."

"And now you have another birthday, Jack," said Mother.

"Dear me! How fast the time goes!"

"And how fast Jack grows," said Father. "You can see that from the pictures."

"Now it is time for you to take my picture again," Jack said. "When can you do it, Father?"

"Well," Father said, "I have to go to work soon. So I don't think I will take the picture until after your party. Is everything ready for the party?"

"Everything but us," Jack said. "You see, we asked the other children to do a funny stunt at the party. And we were going to do one, too. But we just can't think of anything to do."

Father looked at Mother.

And Mother looked at Father.

"Maybe we can help you," they said.

And then Mother went hurrying away.

"It's your birthday, Jack," she said when she came back with three big boxes. "But we have something here for all of you. It will be more fun that way."

"Whee-ee!" said Jack, as he looked in his box. "Cowboy clothes!"

"That is what I have, too," said Sue.

"Me, too," Tommy said. "Me, too."

"Oh, thank you," said Jack. "This will help us. Now I know a stunt we can do. A good cowboy stunt!"

Fun at the Party

Jack had his party outdoors, out under the big trees in the yard.

And when the children came, there was a fine lunch all ready for them.

There were hot soup and sandwiches, milk, and apples.

And last of all there was a surprise. A surprise that Mother had made.

After lunch Jack jumped up and said, "Come on! Let's do our stunts."

"Not so fast, Jack," Mother said. "Not so fast. It is not good for you to jump and run just after you eat. Why don't you rest a little first?"

"Oh, no," said Jack. "We are not tired! Come on! It is time for the stunts."

"Oh-h-h!" Don said. "I ate too much. I don't think I can walk now!"

"Well, then," said Jack, "maybe we should rest. But I am not tired."

"Let's all get down and pretend we are sleeping," said Sue. "Mother will tell us when to get up."

"All right," said the others. And soon they were pretending to sleep.

"Z-z-z-z!" said Bill. "Z-z-z-z!"

"Oh, Billy!" laughed Jill. "Stop that."

Soon Mother came and said, "You may do your stunts now."

Up jumped Don and his sister Jill.

"We are ready for the stunts," they said.

Up jumped Bill, Ellen, Sue, and Tommy.

"So are we," they said.

But Jack did not jump up. He did not even look up.

"Well, well!" Mother said. "And this is the boy who was not tired!"

"Look at him," laughed Sue. "Sleeping at his own birthday party!"

"Let's wake him up," said Jill.

"Whee!" said Bill, as he went running over to Jack. "I know a good way to wake him."

But Jack's puppy Spot got there first.

And then Jack did wake up. He waked up in a hurry.

The Three Stunts

"Now the fun starts," said Jack. "Who wants to give the first stunt?"

"Jill and I do," said Don. "But you must all look away until we are ready."

So the others looked away.

Soon Don called, "All ready now," and then the children saw a horse.

Round and round it went.

Galloping, galloping, galloping!

"Oh, ho!" laughed the children. "What a funny old horse!"

"Come on, Ellen," said Bill. "We are next."

"Oh!" laughed Ellen. "Just wait until you see what we are going to do!"

"First you must look away," Bill said. "Don't look at us until we tell you to."

So the children looked away until Bill called, "All ready now."

"Oh, my!" cried Sue in surprise. "What a big man!"

"And what a fat woman!" laughed Jill.

"Three cowboys will lasso some things for you now," Jack said. "We will lasso three little trees over there."

"Ready!" called Sue, and round and round went the lassos. "Go!" she said.

Away went the three lassos.

"Ow-w-w-w-w!" cried Don.

"Let me go," called Ellen.

"Bow-wow-wow!" said Spot.

"Well!" laughed Jack. "We lassoed some things all right. But we didn't lasso the right ones!"

Father Takes a Picture

Father came home just after the party was over.

"Oh, Daddy!" said Jack. "I wish you had come in time to see our stunt."

"It was funny," said Sue. "Everyone laughed and laughed at us."

"Well, well," Father said, as he went hurrying into the house, "I got here just in time to take your picture. Wait right here, and I'll take it as soon as I come out."

"Now," said Father when he came out, "see if you can look like cowboys. Are you ready?"

"All ready," said Jack.

"Ready," said Sue.

"Me, too," said Tommy.

Then Father took the picture.

Three days after that the children saw it, and this is how they looked.

Jack and the New Neighbors

Good-by to Bill and Ellen

"What are you doing?" asked Jack.

"I am making something to give to Ellen," Sue said. "She and Bill are going away to live on a farm."

"Yes, I know," Jack said. "But why do you have to give her something?"

"Oh, Jack," cried Sue, "I don't HAVE to give her something! I want to. Then she will know I like her and I will miss her."

"I see," said Jack.

"You know," Sue went on, "Ellen likes my doll with the toy basket. So I am making her one just like it."

Then Jack began to do some thinking.

"I like Bill," he thought. "And I am going to miss him. I guess I will buy something for him."

So Jack went to the toy store.

When he came home, he had a boat for Bill.

But the more he looked at that boat the more he wanted to keep it.

"I know what I will do," he thought at last. "I will keep the toy boat and give my water color paints to Bill. They are old paints, and I don't want them any more."

Soon Jack and Sue were ready to go next door.

But just as they started to go out of the house, they met Bill and Ellen.

"Hello," called Sue in surprise. "We were on our way to see you."

"We wanted to give you something and to say good-by," said Jack.

"How funny!" laughed Ellen. "We were coming to give you something and to tell you good-by."

"You always liked my white mouse, Jack," said Bill. "So now he is yours. Your mother says you may have him."

"And this little plant is for you, Sue," said Ellen. "It is the best one I had."

"Thank you!" cried Sue and Jack.

"You are very welcome," said Ellen.

"Now," said Sue, "this box is for you, Ellen, and the other one is for Bill. But don't look in the boxes until you get to the farm."

"Thank you!" said Ellen. "We want to look now, but we won't."

Then the children all said good-by, and Bill and Ellen left for home.

As they started down the walk, Jack came puffing after them.

"Wait!" he called. "Give me back that little white box, Bill, and take this big blue one. There is something in it you will really like."

What do you think was in the blue box?

The New Neighbors

"Look, Sue," said Jack. "Look! Our new neighbors are here."

"I can't see any of the neighbors," said Sue. "But I can see their things out there."

"Oh, look!" said Jack. "I think they must have chickens in that one big box. What do you think is in the other one?"

"I don't know," said Sue. "But if we wait and see, maybe we will find out."

"I guess so," said Jack. "But that isn't what I really want to find out. I want to know if our new neighbors have any children."

"Oh, so do I!" said Sue. "Won't it be fun if they have? And maybe they have some pets like a dog or a cat. I just can't wait to find out."

"Well," Jack said, "I think I will go out and play. Maybe I will see some of our new neighbors out there.

Come on, Tommy. You can come along, too."

Soon Jack and Tommy came in again.

"Oh, Sue!" called Jack. "A boy and a girl are going to live next door to us. They are about as old as we are."

"Baby, too," said Tommy.

"Yes," Jack said. "A baby, too."

"How do you know?" asked Sue.

"We just know," laughed Jack. "And if you look out there now, you will see how we know."

Something for the Family

The children were so busy talking about the new neighbors that they didn't see Father come home.

They didn't see the big box he had with him.

"My!" said Father, as he put down the box. "This weighs more than I thought it did!"

"Oh!" cried Sue. "What is that?"

"Something for all of us," said Father, as he opened the box. "Something we have been wanting."

"Whee!" cried Jack. "Now we can all get weighed!"

"Weigh us now, Daddy," said Sue.

"All right," said Father. "Hop on, and I'll weigh you."

First he weighed Sue. He said she weighed 79 pounds.

Next he weighed Jack. He said Jack weighed 63 pounds.

"I weigh 63 pounds this time," said Jack. "But next time I'll weigh even more. You just wait and see!"

"You won't weigh more if you don't eat what you should," said Sue.

Just then Tommy said, "Weigh me!"

"Hop on, Tommy," said Father. "Let's see what a big boy like you will weigh."

Then Father said, "42 pounds! Why, that can't be right. That is enough for two to weigh!"

"Oh, ho!" laughed Jack. "You DID weigh two, and you didn't know it. You weighed Tommy and Spot!"

WEIGHT CHART

	SEPT.	OCT.	NOV.	DEC.	JAN.	FEB.	MAR.	APR.	MAY	JUN
SUE	79 lb.									
JACK	63 lb.									
TOMMY	37 lb.									
SPOT	5 lb.									
FATHER	185 lb.									
MOTHER	136 lb.									

How Much Do You Weigh?

Here is something that Jack made for all the family to see.

What can you find out when you look at this?

Why do you think it was a good plan for Jack to make this?

When were you weighed last?

How many pounds did you weigh then?

How would a plan like Jack's help you know if you weigh more now than the last time you were weighed?

The New Boy

"It is a fine day," said Mother. "You should be outdoors, Jack."

"I know," said Jack. "I am going over to Don's right now. Some of us are going to play ball in his back yard."

"Why don't you ask the new boy next door to go, too?" asked Mother.

"I would ask him," Jack said. "But do you know what, Mother? He throws a ball with his left hand. I saw him in the yard this morning.

So he would not be good enough to play with us."

"Why, Jack!" Mother said. "Some of the best ball players throw with their left hands. Didn't you know that?"

"No-o," said Jack. "I didn't know that. But I'll ask him to play with us if you say so."

Then Jack went to find the new boy.

"Hello," he said when he found him. "I am Jack Foster."

"Hello," said the new boy. "I am Sam White, and this is my new wagon."

"Would you like to play ball with some of us in Don's yard?" asked Jack.

"Yes, thanks," said Sam. But he thought, "Oh, dear! I don't want to. It won't be much fun playing with boys I don't know."

When the boys came to Don's yard, Jack said, "Hello, everyone. This is Sam White. He lives next door to me."

"Hello," said Don and Tom and Johnnie.

"We can use another player," said Dick.

Then Don said, "Here is my new ball, Sam. Let's see you throw it."

Up went Sam's left hand. Then WHIZ! The ball went flying over to Don.

"Whew!" cried Don in surprise. "You can really throw, can't you!"

The boys played until dinner time, and then they started for home.

"Come and play with us every day," Don called after Sam.

As he pushed Jack home in the wagon, Sam thought, "Jack and Don are lots of fun, and so are Tom, Dick, and Johnnie. I am glad I came to play with them even if I didn't want to at first."

Jack was doing some thinking, too.

"Playing ball is more fun now that Sam is here," he thought. "I guess Mother was right. Some of the best ball players really DO throw with their left hands!"

A Busy Street

The next morning Jack went to see if Sam was ready for school.

"I'll show you a fast way to get to school," Jack said to Sam as they started out.

"But there is one street where we have to look out. The cars go fast there, and we have to be very careful."

Soon the boys came to a busy street.

"Is this where we must be careful?" asked Sam.

"Yes," said Jack. "We must look first to the left and then to the right. If cars are coming, we must stand and wait."

Just then a car went HONK! HONK!

"Whew!" said Jack. "We have to look behind us, too!"

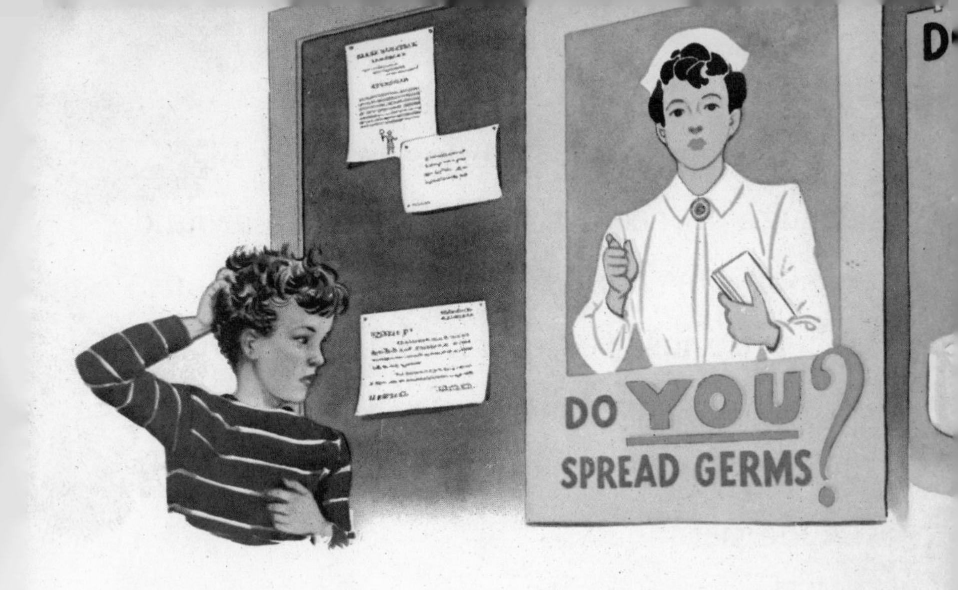

A Morning at School

The first thing that the children saw at school was a big sign.

Jack read it carefully. Then he said, "What are germs, Miss Williams?"

"There are some germs on your hands right now, Jack," said Miss Williams.

"Where?" asked Jack. "I don't see any germs."

"They are there anyway," Miss Williams said. "Even if you can't see them."

Then she said, "Germs are not big enough to see. But they are all around us—on our hands, on our toys, and on other things we see and use every day.

Some germs make us sick, and that is why we don't want to let them get inside us."

"How can we keep germs that make us sick from getting inside us?" Jack asked.

"Look at the other two signs," said Miss Williams. "They will tell you."

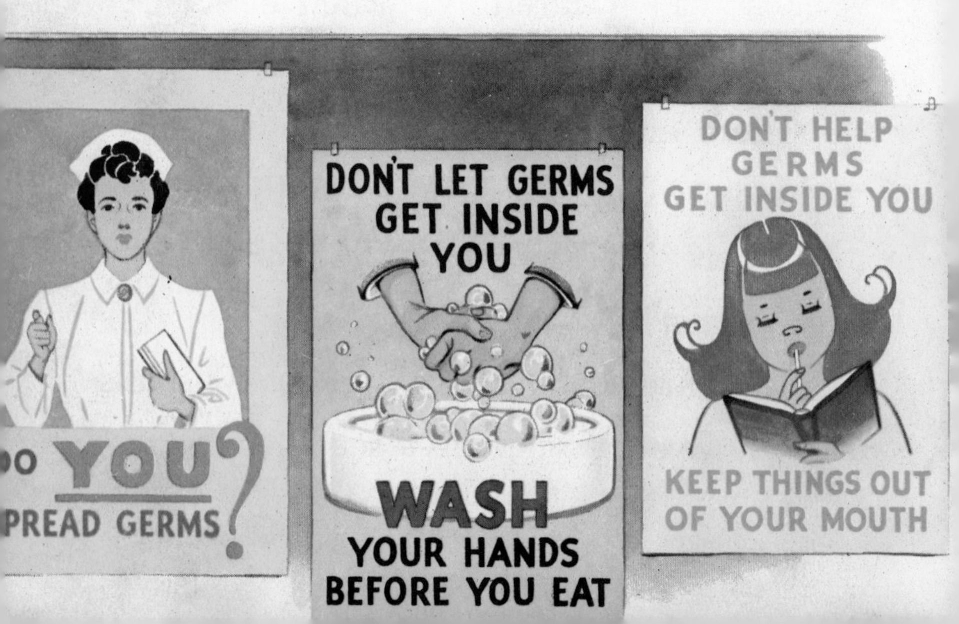

"I don't think I spread germs," said Jack. "I don't, do I?"

"Look around you this morning," said Miss Williams. "You will soon find out if you and your friends spread germs."

So Jack looked around him all morning. Here are some things that he saw.

Did Jack see any children spreading germs? What were they doing?

What can you do to keep from spreading germs?

Jack's Plan

Every day before it was time to eat, Mother would say, "Are your hands clean, Jack? Did you wash them with hot water and lots of soap?"

And very often Jack would have to say, "Well, I didn't this time, but next time you won't have to tell me."

That is the way things were until Jack found out about germs.

Then he thought to himself, "If I don't wash before I eat, I may eat some germs. And I don't want to do that."

So Jack thought of a plan to make him think to wash his hands.

And he used his plan that very day.

"Look, Sue," he said. "These will make me think to wash before I eat."

"Oh, ho!" laughed Sue. "How can two old paper hands do that?"

"If I think to wash before I eat, I'll put up the paper hands this way," said Jack.

"If Mother has to tell me, I'll put them up this way. The black hands will make me think to wash next time!"

The Plant and the Mouse

After school one day Jack and Sue were playing with their new neighbors.

Sue was telling Jane about her plant.

"I keep it in my own room," she said. "My, but it is pretty!"

"I wish I could see it," said Jane.

"You can," Sue said. "Come home with me, and I'll show it to you."

Jack was busy telling Sam about his new pet, the white mouse.

"Bill named him Poky," he said. "But he really isn't poky. He lives in a box with a toy merry-go-round in it. And he makes that merry-go-round go round and round all day long!

Come home with me and see him."

When the children got home, Jack and Sue ran to get the plant and the mouse.

Soon they came back, but they were not running any more. And they didn't look very happy.

"Why, Sue!" said Jane. "Is THAT the pretty plant you were telling about?"

"What is the matter with your mouse?" asked Sam. "He looks sick to me."

Just then Mother came along.

"Look, Mother," said Jack. "Look! Sue's plant isn't pretty and green any more, and Poky won't run or play on his toy merry-go-round or anything! What do you think is the matter?"

"Well, now," said Mother, "let's stop and think. Have you been watering your plant and seeing that it gets sunlight, Sue? And you, Jack—"

"Oh, dear!" cried Jack. "I didn't feed Poky this morning. And I didn't put his box in the sunlight.

Now I know why he won't run or play!"

So Jack and Sue got busy.

Sue got some water for her plant, and then she put it in the sunlight.

And Jack got food and water for his pet.

"Well," said Jane, "I was reading the other day that plants and animals must have food, water, and sunlight. If they don't get them, they just can't be strong and healthy. Now I know that is so."

"If you will come here and look," Mother said, "you can see some others who must have food, water, and sunlight to make them strong and healthy."

"Oh!" laughed the children, as they looked. "We are the other ones!"

Ready or Not?

One Saturday as Jack jumped out of bed, he thought, "This is the day Sam and I are going to the football game with Daddy.

And here I am sleeping late! I must hurry and get ready."

So he got ready in a hurry.

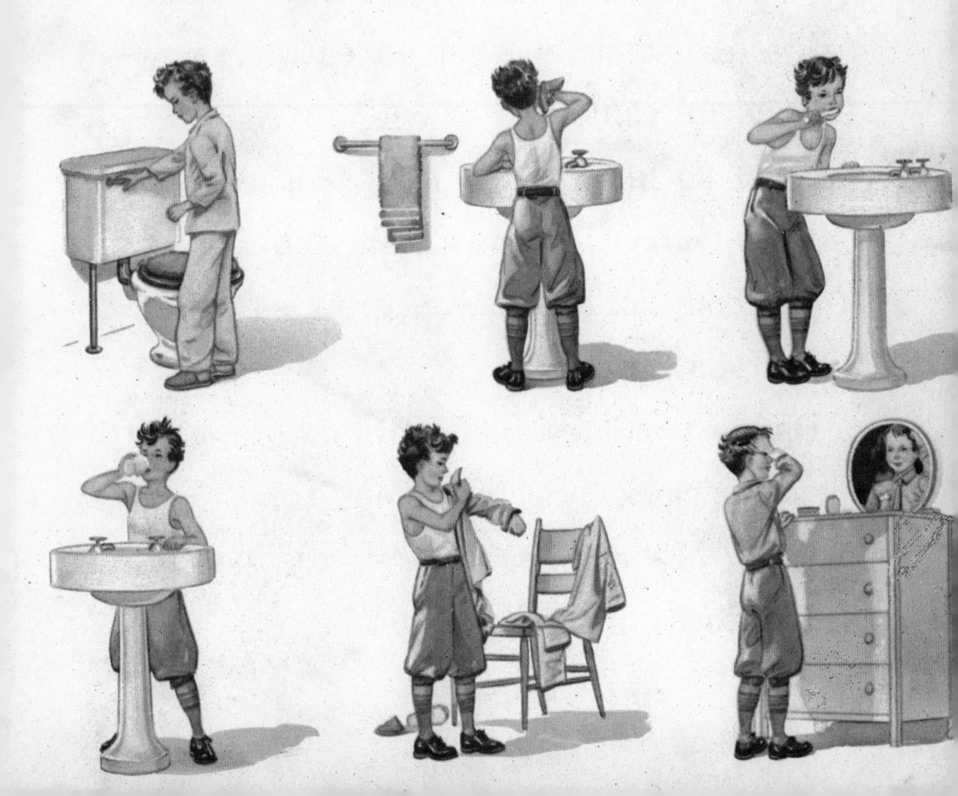

At breakfast Jack began to eat as fast as he could.

"What's your hurry?" asked Sue.

"I must be ready when Daddy comes," said Jack, and he went on eating as fast as he could.

"Not so fast, Jack," said Mother. "It isn't good for you to eat too fast. Your food can't help you grow so well when you do that.

Daddy won't be home from work until eleven o'clock. So take your time."

"Yes, Mother," said Jack, and he began to eat a little slower.

After breakfast Jack thought, "It is just about eleven o'clock. I'll wait here at the window until Daddy gets home."

After he had waited a little, there was a HONK, HONK, HONK outdoors.

Jack ran to see if it could be his father. But it was only one of the neighbors.

So he waited some more.

At last he said, "I'll go and see if Sam is ready, Mother. I'll be right back."

HONK, HONK, HONK went a car.

This time it really was Father, and Sam was out there with him.

But there was no sign of Jack.

He had not been to Sam's house, and Sam didn't know where he could be.

"How funny!" said Mother. "He just left, and he said he would be right back."

Just then Jack called from somewhere, "Daddy! Sam! Wait for me! Don't go without me! I am all ready."

"If he is all ready, why doesn't he come?" asked Father. But he and Sam went to see anyway.

And then they found out why!

Off to the Football Game

"This is going to be a good game," said Father, as he and the boys started off in the car. "A very good game."

"I know it will be," said Jack. "I just can't wait to see it."

"Are you hungry?" asked Father. "We can eat soon if—" But all at once he stopped talking and stopped the car.

"Look at that boy!" cried Sam. "He didn't stop for the red light."

A little later Jack saw some girls walking in the road, and he asked, "Why don't they keep to the right?"

Father said, "When you are in a car, you should keep to the right of the road. But when you walk on the road, you keep to the left. Can you see why?"

"No," Jack said, "I can't see why."

"I can," said Sam. "If you walk at the right of the road, you can't see any of the cars behind you. They may run into you from the back."

The car went down the road a way, and then Father began to go slower.

"If you hurry, you won't have to stop here," said Jack.

"Now, Jack!" Father said. "We are not going to hurry so much that we can't be careful."

"We might get hurt if we didn't stop here," said Sam. "And I don't want to get hurt. I want to get to that game!"

The Football Game

Father, Jack, and Sam had lunch and got to the game before it started.

"I wish the game would start," said Jack. "I just can't wait to see it!"

"This is the first time I have been to a football game," said Sam. "It is going to be fun for me, all right."

Just then a man came along.

"Candy!" he called. "Buy it here!"

"I have some pennies," said Jack. "I am going to buy some candy."

Then the people next to Sam got some fruit, sandwiches, and candy.

"We can't eat all of this candy," said one woman to Sam. "You boys take some, too. Take all you want."

At last the game started.

And then the boys were very busy.

Busy looking at the game, and busy eating candy!

When the game was over, Father said, "I have a surprise for you. We are going to stop at Grandfather's farm for a chicken dinner."

"Oh-h!" cried Jack. "Why did I eat all that candy? Now I may not have any room for Grandmother's dinner!"

"Oh, dear!" said Sam. "I ate too much, too. Now I don't feel hungry."

"My!" said Father. "I was looking at the game, and I didn't see what you ate. What will your Grandmother say!"

"I know," laughed Jack. "She will look at all three of us and say, 'My, my, my! You are all old enough to know better!' "

"And so we are," laughed Father. "And so we are!"

One Rainy Day

Splash, splash, splash went Jack as he walked along.

Swish, swish, swish went Sam.

"Whee!" called Jack. "This is as good as going for a swim."

"Quack, quack, quack!" said Sam. "That is duck talk for 'Yes, it is.'"

"Oh, ho!" laughed Jack. "I guess I will talk duck talk, too. If we play in the water like ducks, we should talk like ducks."

"We have to go in Miss Peters' house now," said Sam. "She is going to give us our lunch today. Our mothers went away and won't be home until later."

"Quack, quack!" said Jack. "I know."

Just then Miss Peters saw them.

"Boys!" she called from her window. "What are you doing?"

"Quack, quack, quack, quack," said Sam. "That means 'pretending we are ducks.' "

"Well, you are not ducks," Miss Peters said. "And you are getting your feet all wet. Don't you know better than that? Why, you may get a cold doing that!"

"Well-ll," said Sam. "Well——"

"Well," said Miss Peters, "I think you should hurry in here and get dry."

So the boys went in, and Miss Peters helped them take off their wet shoes.

"Keeping on wet shoes is not good for you," she said.

Then she put their shoes to dry and gave the boys their lunch.

When they left for school, she gave them an umbrella and some old overshoes.

"Quack, quack," said Sam. "Thank you."

"Quack, quack, quack, quack, quack," said Jack. "That means 'Now we really are ducks.' Ducks who can go walking in the water."

Playing with Clay

"I have some new clay," said Jane one day. "Let's make clay animals."

"Oh!" said Sue. "I know how to do that, and I'll show you how."

"All right," said Jane. "I'll make a cat like Puff and a bird in a nest."

"I'll make a fat little pony," said Sam.

"I'll make a squirrel," said Jack. "A squirrel with a long, long tail."

"Oh, no, you won't," said Sue. "You must make just what I tell you to make. You must all make a cow."

Then Sue said, "Now I want all of you to take a little ball of clay for the cow's head. Make it look just like this."

Jane and Sam did what Sue said that they should do.

But Jack thought, "I don't think I want to make the cow's head that way. I know another way to make it."

So Jack made the head his own way.

"Now," said Sue, "take a big ball of clay and make it look just like this."

And that is what Jane and Sam did.

But Jack thought of another way.

And so it went. Sue showed them all just what to do, and they did what she showed them.

All of them but Jack!

At last three of the cows were made.

When Sam looked at them, he said, "I can't tell which cow is the one that I made. My cow looks just like yours, Jane. And our two look just like Sue's."

"Jack," said Sue, "is yours ready?"

"Well-ll," said Jack, "I guess so. But I didn't make it the way you did."

When the children saw Jack's cow, they all began to laugh.

"Oh, Jack!" said Sue. "We like your cow best of all."

Sue and Her Friends

A Beauty Shop at Home

"Oh, look!" said Sue. "There is Tom Hill's sister coming out of the beauty shop. My, but she looks pretty!"

"Hm-m!" said Jane. "I guess I'll go to the beauty shop next Saturday. My mother will let me. I know she will."

"I am going to the beauty shop, too," said Nancy.

"So are we," said Jill and her sister Patty.

"Oh, dear!" thought Sue. "I don't think I can go."

But she didn't want to say that.

So she said, "I am going to let them fix my hair at the beauty shop, too. I'll be seeing you there on Saturday."

When Saturday came, Sue was not very happy.

"Here I am," she was thinking, "the only girl in town who can't go to the beauty shop to get her hair fixed!

The only one who has to have her hair washed at home!"

Just then Jane came to the door.

"Hello, Jane! Come in," said Sue. "But don't stop if you are on your way to the beauty shop. I—well, I—"

"Oh!" said Jane. "I am not going there. I just thought I was going."

R-r-r-r! Someone was at the door.

And when Sue opened it, she saw Nancy Bird and Jill and Patty Green.

"Hello there, come in," said Sue. "Jane is here, too. But we are not going to the beauty shop with you. Not today anyway."

"Well-ll," said Jill. "We, well-ll—"

"You see," said Patty, "we can't go. We just thought we could. Our mothers won't let us go. They say we are not old enough."

"I'll tell you what," said Sue. "Let's have a beauty shop here."

So that is what they did, and Mother came and helped. She showed them how to wash hair like this.

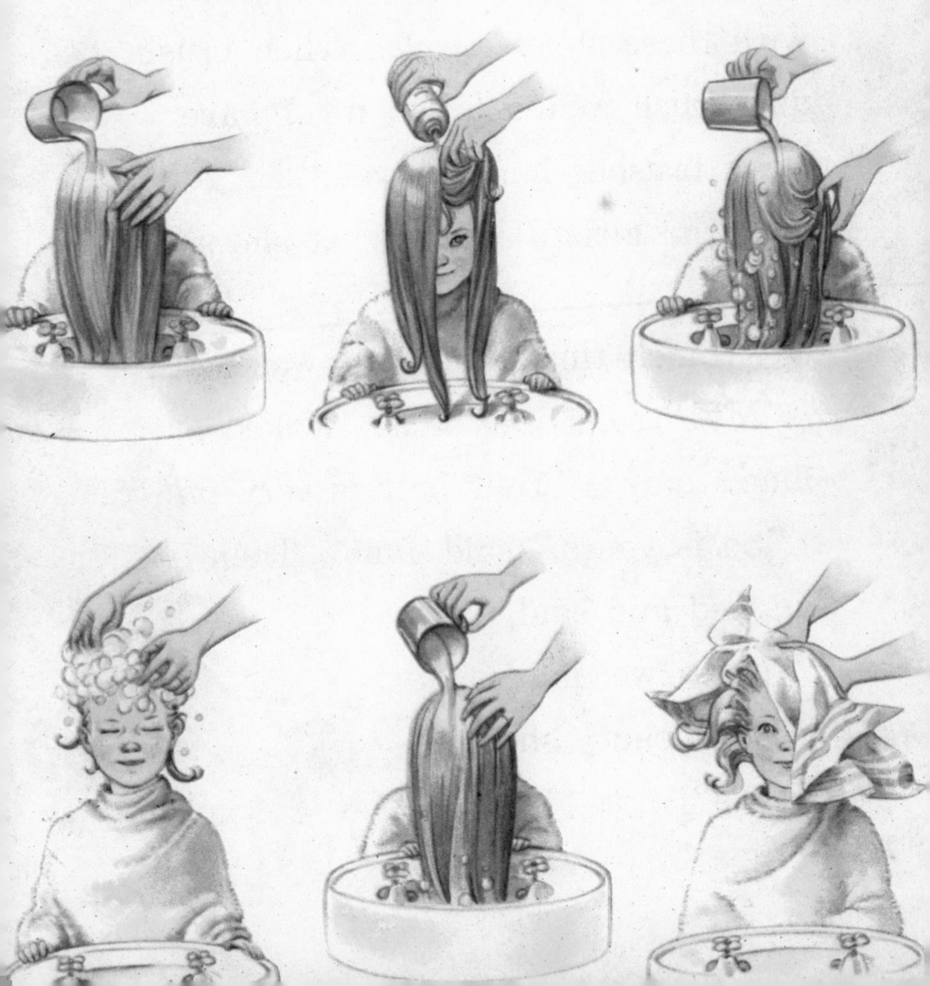

Then the children began to wash one another's hair.

"This is fun," Jill said. "After this I'll wash my own hair every week."

"Now," said Mother when the heads had all been washed, "dry your hair with these clean towels. Then brush it and brush it and brush it. I have clean brushes here for you."

So the girls did just what she said.

At lunch time their hair was dry.

"My!" said Sue, as she looked at Jane's hair. "Your hair is very pretty!"

"So is yours," said Jane. Then she laughed and said,

"I guess we didn't need a beauty shop, did we?"

Father's Pictures

"Here is a picture of you, Sue," said Father. "I took it the other day when you didn't see me."

"Do I really look like that?" cried Sue, as she looked at the picture.

"Oh, Daddy, why didn't you tell me before you took my picture? Then I could have been standing straight."

"If you want to grow straight, you must stand and walk as straight as you can all the time," said Father.

"Don't do it just when I am going to take your picture."

"Look here, Sue," said Jack. "See how straight I can be when I walk. I'll walk with a book on my head, and it won't fall off.

Look at me now! See how straight I can walk!"

"You are walking straight now," laughed Father. "But the other day I took a picture of you, too. I took it when you didn't see me, Jack.

And you should see how you were walking then!"

"Oh, my!" said Jack when he saw his picture. "Don't I look funny here! I have been telling Sue how to walk straight, but I should have been telling ME."

Growing Straight

After they saw Father's pictures, Sue and Jack thought more about standing as straight as they could.

What are they doing here that will help them grow straight?

What can you do that will help you grow straight?

Vegetable Surprises

Jill and Patty Green were coming to dinner, and Mother and Sue were busy getting ready for them.

"What vegetables do Jill and Patty like?" asked Mother.

"Oh, let's not have any vegetables for dinner," said Sue. "Jill and Patty don't like them."

"We must have vegetables," Mother said: "We should eat some vegetables every day. They make strong bones and healthy teeth for us. Don't Jill and Patty know that?"

"I don't know," said Sue. "I just know they don't like vegetables and won't eat them if they can help it."

Then Mother thought of a good plan.

"Sue," she said, "why don't we fix our vegetables a new way? Jill and Patty may be surprised to see how good they are."

So Mother and Sue got busy, and this is how they fixed one of the vegetables.

Next Mother got some other vegetables and showed Sue how to make something funny. This is what it was.

At five o'clock Jill and Patty came.

Soon everyone sat down to eat.

"See the vegetable man I made for you," Sue said to Jill.

"Oh, yes!" laughed Jill. Then she started to say, "But I won't eat it. I don't like——"

But all at once she thought, "Sue and her mother worked and worked to make this. I'll just have to eat it."

Patty was thinking that, too. So the two girls began to eat.

And what a surprise! It was good!

Then Mother said, "Here is something you will like, too. Have some of it."

Jill and Patty took what she gave them and thought, "We must eat this even if we don't like it."

Soon Patty said, "M-m-m-m! This is very good. What is it?"

"I know one thing about it," said Jill. "It is not a vegetable. It is much too good to be a vegetable!"

"Oh, but it is a vegetable!" said Sue's mother. "It really is."

"Well, what do you know about that!" laughed Jill. "We were eating a vegetable and didn't know it!"

"You liked it, too," laughed Sue. "That shows you really do like vegetables. You just think you don't."

Sue's Book about Foods

"Mother, do you want to see a book I made at school?" asked Sue. "It tells about milk and eggs and lots of other foods that are good for us to eat. It has pictures in it, too."

"Why, Sue!" said Mother. "What a pretty book! I think I'll take time to read it right now."

So Mother began to read the book that Sue had made.

This is what Sue had put in her book about foods that help make strong bones and healthy teeth.

Why do we need strong bones and healthy teeth?

What are the names of some foods that will help make them for us?

This is what Sue had put in her book about other good foods to eat.

What are the names of some foods that help make strong muscles for us?

What are the names of some foods that help us grow and keep well?

Sue Always Knows

"Take your winter coat today, Jack," said Sue. "It is going to be very cold at lunch time, and you will need it."

"Mother," said Jack, "I don't need my winter coat, do I? It isn't very cold."

Mother said, "Maybe Sue is right, Jack. Maybe you will need that coat before the day is over."

Sue was right. At lunch time there was a strong, cold wind. And Jack was glad he had his winter coat with its big warm pockets.

Two days later Sue said, "It is going to rain today, Jack. It will be a wet, cold day. You will need a raincoat, overshoes, and maybe an umbrella."

"It is not going to rain," said Jack. "You don't always know about cold and rain and everything, Sue."

"Oh, yes, I do," laughed Sue. "You just wait and see."

Once again Sue was right. It was raining after school, and Jack had to stand in the doorway until the rain had stopped.

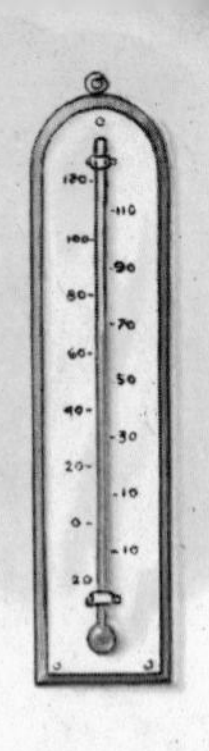

That night Jack said to Father, "How can you tell how hot or how cold it is?"

"Well," said Father, as he showed Jack a thermometer, "you can always look at this."

Then Father said, "Your mother and I use this thermometer to help us know if the house is too hot or too cold.

We have a thermometer outside, too. You can see it out there by the window. It tells us how hot or how cold it is outdoors."

"Can a thermometer tell how cold it will be the next day?" asked Jack. "Can it tell us when it will rain?"

"Oh, no," said Father. "A thermometer tells us how warm or how cold it is at the time we look at it. That is all."

"Well, then," said Jack, "how can Sue always tell when it is going to rain or get cold?"

"Why don't you ask her?" Father said.

So Jack asked Sue.

She only laughed and said, "Oh, I just know! Maybe someday I'll tell you how I know."

"Make her tell me, Mother," cried Jack.

But Mother only said, "You can find out if you will get up early one of these mornings."

"Get up early?" thought Jack. "How can that help me find out? Oh well, I'll do it anyway."

Early next morning Jack ran down the stairs to see what he could see.

A little later Sue came down and went hurrying over to the radio.

At breakfast Jack asked, "Will I need my winter coat today, Sue?"

"Yes, you will," said Sue. "There will be a strong, cold wind today."

"How do you know?" asked Jack.

"Oh, I always know," laughed Sue.

"I know now, too," laughed Jack. "And I won't tell YOU how I know."

How Can You Find Out?

Why do you need to know how warm or cold it is outdoors in the morning?

Why do you need to know if it may rain or snow before the day is over?

There are many ways by which you can find out these things.

What are some of these ways?

Sue and the Radio

After lunch one Saturday Jack jumped up and said, "I think I'll go out and play now, Mother. I'll be back a little later."

"Oh, Jack!" said Mother. "Please rest a little before you go out to play."

"All right," said Jack, as he sat down by the radio, "I'll rest. I want to hear something on the radio anyway."

Then Jack got a program on the radio called "Time to Laugh."

Soon he was laughing so much that Mother and Father came to hear the program, too.

All three of them were laughing when Sue came into the room.

She went hurrying over to the radio and put on another program.

"Say!" cried Jack. "Why did you do that, Sue?"

"The program I want to hear is just coming on," said Sue.

"Now see here, Susan," said Father. "Three of us have a program we want to hear very much. You are the only one who wants another program. So what do you think we should do?"

"Father wants me to say I'll put back the program they all want to hear," thought Sue. "Well, I'll do it, but I don't want to."

So Sue put back the program called "Time to Laugh." But she didn't look at all happy.

She sat in her chair and looked just as angry as angry could be.

Before long someone on the radio said something funny. And soon Sue was laughing just as much as all the others were.

"My!" she thought. "This is more fun than the program that I wanted to hear. And now I am glad that I didn't have my own way about the radio!"

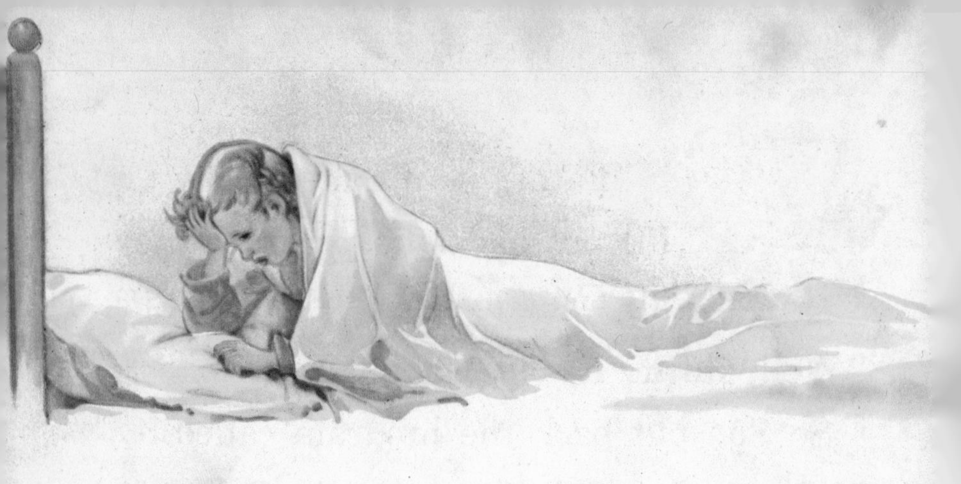

Sue's Cold

"Sue!" called Mother. "Oh, Sue! I have called and called you. It is time you were up."

"Oh!" thought Sue. "My head hurts! I don't think I can get up today."

But just then she thought of the fun her friends were going to have at school.

"This is the day of the puppet show," she thought. "And I don't want to miss it. Maybe my head will stop hurting soon. Maybe I'll be all right. I guess I'll get up after all."

"Kerchoo!" went Sue, as she got out of bed. "Kerchoo! Kerchoo!"

"Oh, dear!" she thought. "Maybe I am getting a cold. I guess I'll have to take some paper handkerchiefs with me today."

Then she began to get ready for school. Here are the things she did.

When Sue came downstairs to eat breakfast, Mother said, "We didn't wait for you. You are late this morning."

"I know," said Sue, "but after this I'll be on time."

Then she looked at her breakfast.

"Oh, my!" she thought. "I don't want all this food. I don't feel hungry."

"Sue," said Mother, "you don't look very well. Do you feel all right?"

"Oh, I think so," said Sue. "I am just in a hurry to get to school. We are going to see a puppet show today."

On the way to school Sue's head hurt, and the sun hurt her eyes. When she got to school, she was very tired.

She thought, "I should go home. But if I do, I'll miss the puppet show."

In school she sat up very straight and pretended that her head did not hurt.

Soon it was time for the puppet show.

Everyone laughed and laughed at the puppets. Everyone but Sue!

Her head hurt so much now that she could not even look at the puppets.

When the show was over, Miss Gray saw Sue with her head in her hands.

"Why, Susan Foster!" she said. "I think you must be sick."

"Yes," said Sue, "I think I am."

"Well, then," said Miss Gray, "let's go to see the nurse. She will help you."

When the nurse had looked at Sue, she said, "You have a cold, Susan, and you should be home in bed. You need lots of sleep and rest to get over your cold.

You should not be here at school. You may give your cold to others."

"Oh, dear!" said Sue. "I wish I had not come today. I wish I were in bed."

Then the nurse said, "Get your coat and hat. I'll take you home in my car. You will be in bed before you know it!"

Before long Sue was home in bed.

Mother gave her something good to drink, and then she said, "Sleep as much as you can today, Sue. Sleep and good fruit drinks will help make that cold of yours go away."

"Mother," said Sue, "school is fun when I am feeling well. But when I am sick, home is the very best place to be!"

How Do We Get Colds?

When Father came home that night, he was surprised to find Sue in bed.

"Mother says you have a cold," he said. "How did you get it?"

"I don't know," said Sue. "How do we get colds, Daddy?"

"We don't always know," Father said. "But sometimes we do things that may help colds get started.

Why just today I saw some children who may get colds!"

Then Father told her what they had been doing.

Here are some ways Father told about that may help a cold get started.

Sue thought about these ways, and then she said, "Oh, my! I played in the snow without my overshoes the other day. Maybe that helped my cold get started. After this I'll be more careful."

A Plan for Sue

"Sue!" called Jane. "Can you come out?"

"Hello, children," said Mrs. Foster, as she opened the window.

"Sue has a cold, and she has been sleeping late. She will get up soon, but she can't play outdoors. She isn't feeling well enough to do that."

"We can come back later," said Jane. "When Sue gets up, we will come in and play with her."

"I wish I could let you do that," said Mrs. Foster. "But I don't think you should. If you play with Sue, you may get a cold, too."

"Well, then," said Jane, "we won't come in. But you will tell Sue we were here, won't you?"

"Oh, yes," said Mrs. Foster. "I'll tell her as soon as she wakes up."

Then Sue's friends went on down the street.

"My!" said Jill, as they walked along. "It isn't any fun to have a cold and to be inside on Saturday. I wish that we could do something for Sue."

"I know what we can do," said Jane. "We can make a puppet show for her. A new puppet show that no one ever thought of before!"

Then Jane told the others her plan for the puppet show.

"It won't take us very long to get the show ready," she said. "Come on! Let's go over to my house and make the puppets."

So they all went to Jane's house.

There they began to make puppets for the story of "The Three Pigs."

"I'll make the mother pig," said Jill.

"I'll make one little pig," said Sam.

"And I'll make the other little pigs," said Don.

"Well," said Jane, "there is only one animal left for me to make. And you all know what it will be."

Then the children began to work as fast as they could.

This is what they made.

Who Had the Most Fun?

"Oh, dear!" thought Sue. "If I didn't have this cold, I could go out to play. It isn't any fun to be inside all day."

Just then she thought she saw something at the window.

She looked again, and this time she did see something. Three fat little pigs were looking in at her.

Then something big and black came running after them.

"Oh!" laughed Sue. "A puppet show at my window! What fun!"

Down under Sue's window the children were busy working the puppets.

They worked just as fast as they could until at last the show was over.

Then they started home.

As they were going away, Don looked back at Sue's window.

"Oh, look!" he called to the others. "Sue is standing in the window with a sign in her hand. Let's go back and read it."

"I guess Sue liked our show," said Don after he had read the sign.

"I should say she did," Mrs. Foster called from the doorway. "And here is something she wants you to have."

"Cookies!" cried Don.

"Um-m!" said Sam. "Homemade ones!"

"Oh, thank you," said Jill and Jane.

Then Jane said, "We wanted Sue to have some fun today. But I think we had more fun than she did.

We had the most fun of all!"

Fun with Tommy

Who Did It?

"Fell," said Tommy.

"Got hands dirty.

Feet dirty.

Dirty all over.

Have to wash."

Then Tommy went inside to look for Mother, but he didn't see her anywhere. So he went on upstairs.

"Tommy can wash," he said to himself. "Tommy can get clean."

So Tommy washed and washed.

Then he used his towel to dry himself.

The towel got very dirty.

So he used Jack's towel.

"Towel dirty, too," he said, and then he used Sue's towel.

"Dirty, too," he said, and next he used Father's towel.

"Dirty, dirty," he said. Then he saw Mother's towel and used it, too.

"All dry," he said at last. "All clean and dry. All clean and dry now."

Just before dinner Father, Jack, and Sue went upstairs.

Father went to wash first.

He took one look at his towel and cried, "Someone has used my towel!"

Then Jack came running. He took just one look and said, "Someone has used my towel, too."

Then Sue came running. "Oh, look!" she cried. "Someone has used all of our towels. And got them all dirty!"

Mother could hear all this talking. So she came running upstairs.

"Why, Jim!" she cried when she saw Father with his dirty towel. "How did you do that?"

Then she looked at all the other towels.

"Oh, my!" she cried. "How did all of these towels get so dirty?"

"We don't know," said Jack. "We didn't do it."

"Well," said Mother, "if you didn't do it, I know who did."

Now Mother looked for Tommy.

"Tommy!" she called. "Come here."

And when Tommy came, she asked, "Who got these towels all dirty?"

"Tommy did," said Tommy. "Got towels dirty, but got me clean!"

Then Tommy told how he fell down and how he had washed himself.

And Mother began to laugh.

"Tommy, Tommy!" she said. "When you are just a little dirty, you can do the washing. But when you are dirty all over, you must have help!"

"Whew!" said Jack. "You would say more than that to ME if I got all of the towels dirty!"

"I know," said Mother. "But Tommy is just a little boy, and he only wanted to help."

A Plan That Worked Too Well

"Old custard again," said Jack. "Old yellow custard!"

"Why, Jack!" Mother said. "You like custard. You know you do."

"Yes," said Jack. "Only I didn't want it for lunch today. What I really wanted was some homemade cookies. But I'll eat the custard."

So Jack ate all of his custard.

But Tommy didn't eat any.

"Old yellow custard!" he cried. And he pushed the custard away.

"Oh-h-h-h!" thought Jack. "Now see what I did! What will Mother say?"

But Mother only said, "All right, Tommy, drink some more milk then."

She took away the custard and gave Tommy another glass of milk.

After lunch Jack said to Mother, "I didn't think about Tommy when I said 'old yellow custard.' I didn't dream he would say it, too.

And I really do like custard. I was just talking when I said I didn't."

"I know that," said Mother. "But we have to be careful. Tommy thinks we mean what we say. And custard is so good for us! We should all eat it."

"Why is it so good?" asked Jack.

"It is made with milk and eggs," Mother said. "And we need milk and eggs to keep us strong and healthy."

"Is that why you gave Tommy more milk in place of the custard?" asked Jack.

"Yes," said Mother. "We should have three or four glasses of milk a day. If we don't drink the milk, we should eat foods made with milk."

"Well," said Jack, "I didn't know I was getting milk when I ate custard. I thought the only way to get milk was to drink it."

"Now," Mother said, "we must find a way to make Tommy want his custard next time."

So she told Jack about a plan she had.

The very next time there was custard for lunch, Jack said, "Um-m! Custard! My, but it is good! Um-m-m!"

"Um-m!" said Tommy. "Good!"

Then he ate it all and asked for more.

"See, Jack," said Mother, as she gave the last of the custard to Tommy. "See! Our plan worked."

"It worked too well," laughed Jack. "I wanted some more custard, but Tommy is eating it all!"

Getting Enough Milk

Custard is not the only food that is made with milk. These foods are made with milk, too. What are they?

What foods do you sometimes eat that are made with milk?

How much milk should most of us have every day?

Do you get that much milk every day?

Tommy Reads a Story

"Tommy!" cried Sue. "Please don't play right here. I am making something, and you may bump into it."

"Tommy reading," he said. "Tommy not playing."

"Oh!" laughed Sue. "You can look at pictures, but you can't read."

"Can," said Tommy. "Can too read!"

"Well, anyway," Sue said, "would you like me to read you that story?"

"Good," said Tommy. "Sue read."

Sue was just opening the storybook when Mother came along.

"Oh, Sue!" she said. "Please don't read away down there. The light isn't good enough. You may hurt your eyes."

So Tommy and Sue found a chair and sat down to read.

Sue was just opening the storybook again when Father came along.

"Sue," he said, "the light is coming right in your eyes."

Then he fixed the light so that it came on her book and not in her eyes.

"Thank you, Daddy," Sue said. "Now we have a good light."

Then Sue opened the storybook again.

"Why, Tommy!" she said. "We have read you this story over and over. Do you really want to hear it again?"

"Yes," said Tommy. "Hen says——"

But just then all the lights went off!

"What is the matter?" cried Sue.

Father said, "It is the big rain, I guess. If we just wait, the lights will come on again."

"There is nothing to do but wait," said Sue. "We can't read in the dark."

"Tommy can read," said Tommy. And he began, "Hen says cluck, cluck, cluck!

Pig says wee, wee, wee!

Kitten says mew, mew, mew!

Puppy dog says bow-wow-wow!

Duck says quack, quack, quack!

Cow says moo, moo, moo!

Little chicken says peep, peep, peep!"

"Good for you, Tommy," laughed Sue. "You said you could read and you can. You can read even in the dark!"

Shoes That Fit

"I can't make my school shoes look right," said Jack. "I have brushed and brushed them. But they just look old!"

"They are old, Jack," said Mother. "I think you need some new ones."

"Me, too," said Tommy. "Me, too."

"Yes," laughed Mother. "You, too."

Then she said, "Tommy and I will be at the shoe store after school today, Jack. You come there, too, and we will see about getting new shoes."

When Jack got to the shoe store, a man was showing Tommy some shoes.

"These should fit you," he said, as he put some brown shoes on Tommy.

"Pretty!" said Tommy. "Buy them."

"Not so fast, Tommy," said Mother. "We don't really know if they fit you. Walk in them and see how they feel."

So Tommy got up and walked. But all he said was, "Pretty! Buy them, Mama."

"Dear me!" said Mother. "Do you think they really fit him?"

"We can soon find out if they fit," said the man. "A machine here will tell us."

Then he took Tommy to the machine.

"Now," he said to Tommy's mother, "look down."

"See," he went on. "Just see how these shoes give his feet all the room they need. See how they keep the bones in his feet straight."

"All right," said Mother. "We will take these shoes."

Then Jack began to look at shoes.

The first ones he looked at were black. He put them on and began to walk.

"Ow-w!" he cried. "These hurt!"

The man showed him some black and white shoes. But Jack didn't like them at all.

At last he found some light brown and some dark brown shoes that he liked very much. But he didn't know which color to buy.

"Come along to the machine," said the shoe man. "Let's see how your feet look in the dark brown shoes."

Jack got on the machine and looked down at his feet. This is the way they looked.

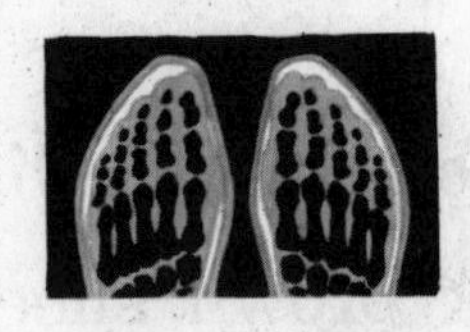

Next he took off the dark brown shoes and put on the light brown ones. Then he got on the machine again. When he looked down, this is what he saw.

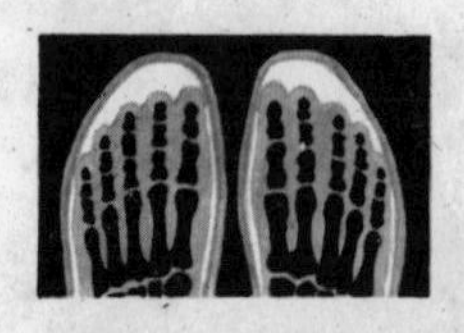

"Oh!" cried Jack. "Now I know which shoes to buy!"

What Is the Matter with Sue?

After dinner that night Jack and Tommy showed Sue their new shoes.

"How do you like them, Sue?" asked Jack.

But Sue didn't say how she liked them.

She didn't say anything at all.

She just walked away.

"Oh!" cried Jack in surprise. "What is the matter with Sue?"

"Jack has new shoes, and Tommy has new shoes," Sue thought, as she walked away. "But I don't have anything new. No one around here buys anything new for me!"

Then she sat down and started to read. But reading was no fun! All she could think of was the boys' new shoes.

The more she thought the more angry she got.

As she sat there, she could hear Mother and Father talking.

All at once Mother said, "Sue will need some new clothes this spring, Jim. She will need a new spring coat and hat before long."

"My!" thought Sue. "And I thought they didn't care about me or my clothes!"

"Oh, dear!" she cried, and she ran over to Mother and Father.

"Jack and Tommy got new things, and I didn't. That is what was the matter with me. Now I wish I had waited before I got so angry!"

"Next time tell us what is the matter right away," said Mother. "You always feel better when you do that."

"You see, Sue," said Father, "we can't all get new things at once. We don't have enough to buy them."

"I see now," said Sue, "but I didn't think of that when I saw the boys with their new shoes."

"Well," said Father, "we all feel left out of things now and then. But most of the time it isn't really so."

"Anyway," said Sue, "you do like me, don't you—even if I did get angry?"

"You know we do," said Father.

Then he laughed and said, "Why, Sue! You are the best girl we have in this family!"

Tommy Goes to a Fire

"Time to take off your play clothes, Tommy," said Sue one Saturday. "Time to put on your clean clothes."

"New shoes, too," said Tommy.

"Yes," said Sue. "New shoes, too."

As Sue was helping Tommy, a red car went flying by the window. WHIZ!

"Whiz!" cried Tommy. "Whiz-z-z-z!"

"Fire!" called Jack from downstairs. "Come on! Let's go to the fire!"

"Hurry, Tommy," said Sue. "Get your shoes on. Hurry now!"

Tommy put on his shoes, and Sue got the coats and hats.

"Wait!" she called. "We are coming, Jack."

"Feet hurt," said Tommy, as they went running to the fire. "Feet hurt!"

"Your shoes are new, Tommy," said Sue. "Maybe that is why they hurt."

"His shoes fit him all right," said Jack. "They can't hurt very much."

Then the children began to run faster and faster.

At last they came to the fire.

"Why, it is Mr. Valentine's old barn!" said Jack. "But it is not burning much."

"How did the fire get started here?" a woman asked a fireman.

"Some boys were playing with fire," said the fireman. "I guess they did it. They ran when they saw us coming."

"I wish I could find the boys who started this fire," said Mr. Valentine. "It might have burned up my barn!"

"And it might have burned up my house, too," said another man. "My house is next door."

"See, Tommy," said Jack, "playing with fire is not safe. So don't ever do it!"

"Playing with fire can make work, too," said Sue. "And every fireman has enough to do as it is."

"Fire out?" asked Tommy. "Fire out?"

"Yes," said Jack. "Let's go home."

"Feet hurt!" said Tommy, as they started home. "Can't walk now."

Then, for the first time, Jack and Sue really looked at Tommy's feet.

The left shoe was on his right foot! And the right shoe was on his left foot!

"Oh, Tommy!" cried Sue. "The fire did that! It made us hurry too much!"

"Come here, Tommy," said Jack. "I'll fix your shoes, and then we will give you a ride home."

What to Do about Fires

That night the children were telling about the fire at Mr. Valentine's barn.

"Some boys started it," said Jack. "They were playing with fire."

"Mr. Valentine said they might have burned up his barn," said Sue.

"The boys might have been burned, too," Mother said.

"Playing with fire is not very safe," said Father. "Many children get hurt that way." And then he told about things that are not safe to do.

Here are some things he told about.

Father told the children other things about fires, too.

He said that they should do one of these things if they ever were the first to see a big fire.

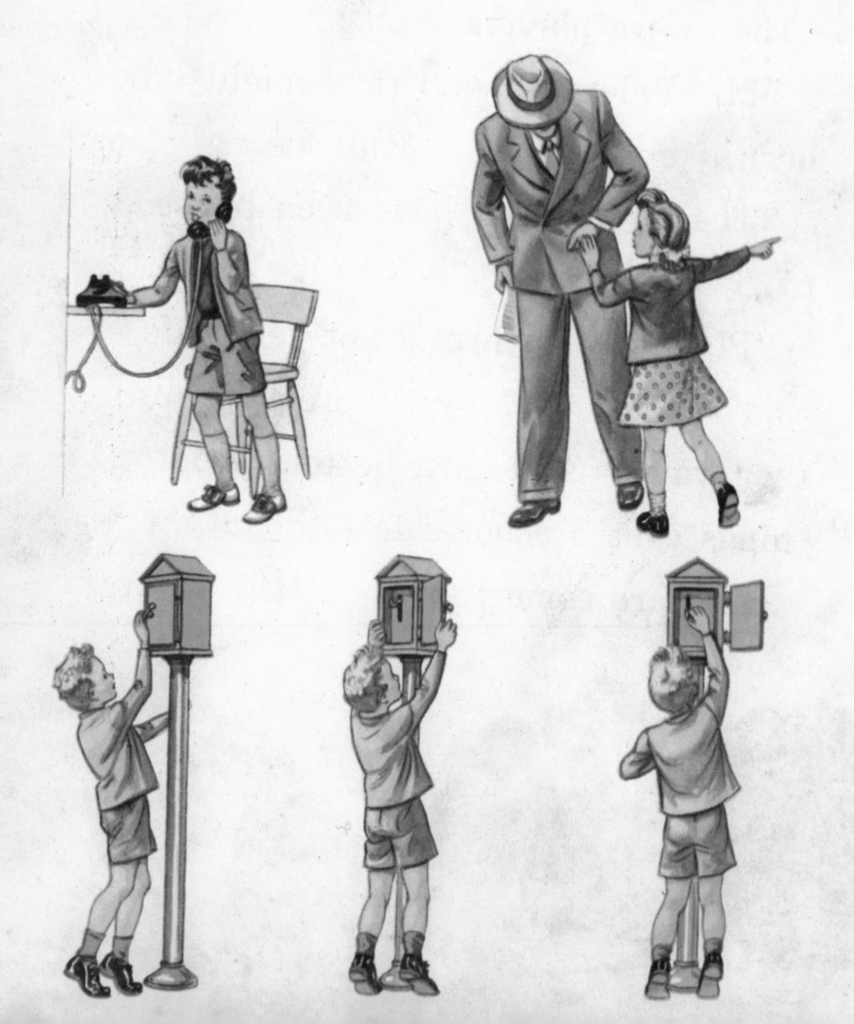

He told them they should know what to do if one of them ever should get his clothes on fire.

He said they should use one of these ways to put the fire out.

Tommy Goes to the Dentist

"Tommy wants to go to the dentist," said Tommy.

"Jack goes to the dentist.

Sue goes to the dentist.

Everyone goes to the dentist.

Tommy wants to go, too."

"He really wants to go, Mother," said Jack. "He knows I am going today, and he wants to go, too."

"Oh, Mother!" laughed Sue. "Isn't Tommy too little to go to the dentist?"

"Not at all," Mother said. "It is time the dentist looked at Tommy's teeth. If he really wants to go today, I think Jack should take him."

So Jack took Tommy with him.

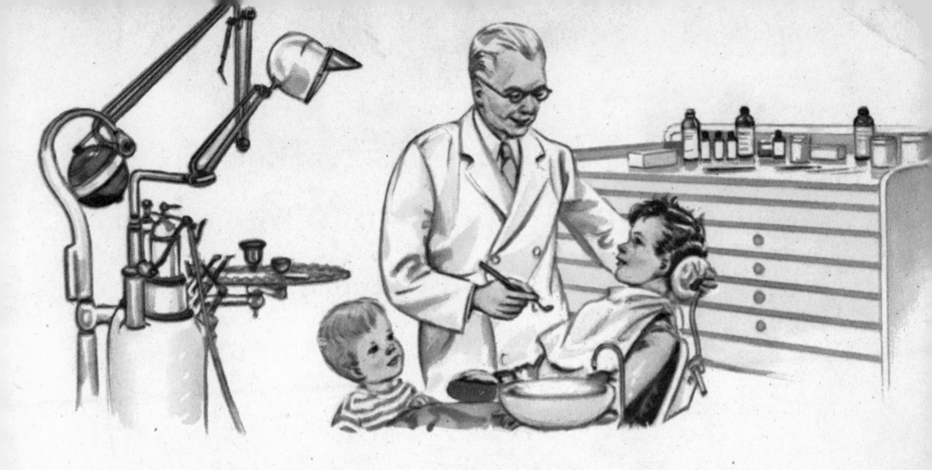

First the dentist looked at Jack's teeth.

"My!" he said. "You take good care of your teeth, Jack. They look fine to me. I'll just clean them for you."

"I do take good care of them," said Jack. "I brush them every morning, and I brush them after I eat."

"I think you do more than that," said the dentist. "I think you must eat lots of fruit and vegetables and drink lots of milk."

"Yes," said Jack, "I do that, too."

Then the dentist cleaned Jack's teeth.

"Now," said the dentist, "hop up here and open your mouth, Tommy. I want to look at your teeth."

So Tommy got up in the chair.

"Teeth white?" he asked.

"Yes, you have fine white teeth, Tommy," the dentist said. "I can't do a thing today to make them any better. But I can give you a ride in this chair. How would you like that?"

"Ride," said Tommy. "Want a ride."

So the dentist made the chair go up, up, up and way, way down.

"Whee!" laughed Tommy. "Whee!"

Next the dentist showed Tommy a little machine.

"Z-z-z!" went the little machine.

"Z-z-z-z!" went Tommy. "Z-z-z!"

At last it was time to go home.

"Good-by, Jack," said the dentist. "Here is a little book for you. It tells how to take good care of your teeth. Good-by, Tommy. Come and see me again some day."

All the way home Jack could hear Tommy saying something. He was saying it over and over.

"Jack goes to the dentist," Tommy was saying.

"Sue goes to the dentist.
Everyone goes to the dentist.
And Tommy goes, too!"

How to Use Your Toothbrush

When Jack got home, he looked at the book that the dentist gave him. In it he saw pictures showing him how to use his toothbrush.

Here are the pictures.

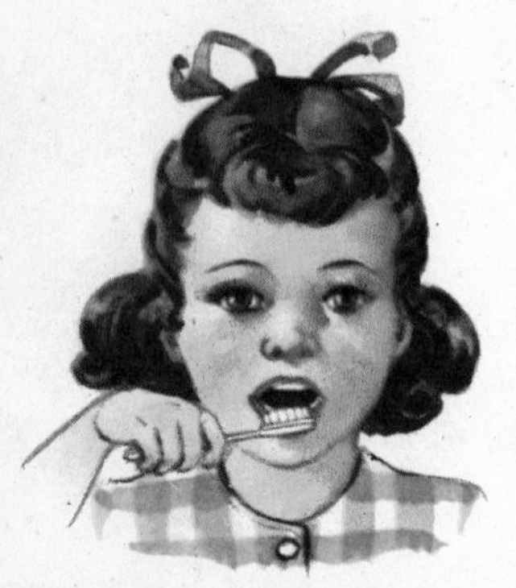

Brush up

Brush down

Brush the teeth on the inside

Keeping Your Teeth Healthy

Which children are eating things that help make strong, healthy teeth?

Which children are doing things that may hurt their teeth?

Tommy and the Needles

"Some needles fell from my basket when I was working here," said Mother. "Will you see if you can find them, Sue? I must go and start our dinner."

"I'll look, but I don't see any," Sue said. "I guess they are lost."

"Look carefully," said Mother. "If you don't find them, Tommy will. And he may put them in his mouth."

So Sue looked, and soon she did find some needles. Three of them!

"Mother has a big old rooster she puts these in," Sue thought. "I'll get it."

So she put the needles down and went to get the rooster from the work basket.

When she came back, the needles were not there! But Tommy was there!

"Tommy!" she cried. "Some needles were here, and now they are gone."

"Um-hum," said Tommy. "All gone."

"Oh!" cried Sue. "Did you take them, Tommy? Did you?"

"Um-hum," said Tommy. "All gone. Put them in——"

But Sue didn't wait to hear any more.

Away she ran to look for Mother.

At the door she bumped into Jack.

"What is the matter with you?" he asked. "Where are you going so fast?"

"Oh, Jack!" cried Sue. "Get Mother! Get a doctor! Do something! I left some needles in the room, and Tommy ate them. I know he did!"

So Jack ran to find Mother.

"What will we do?" cried Sue when she saw Mother coming. "Tommy ate some needles. Three of them!"

"Oh!" said Mother. "Do you know he did? Do you really know? Did you see him do it?"

"No, I didn't see him," Sue said. "But the needles are gone. And he said he ate them."

"No," Tommy said. "Didn't eat any!"

"Well, then, where are they?" asked Mother. "Are they in your pocket? What did you do with them?"

"Tommy helped," said Tommy.

"Pushed them in.
Just like Mother.
Pushed them in.
But not in Rooster.
Pushed them in Bunny Rabbit. See!
All three needles.
Pushed in Bunny Rabbit."

Bedtime

"Tommy is in bed," said Mother. "And now your father and I are going to see Mr. and Mrs. White. If you need anything, call us next door."

"Do Sue and I have to go to bed when we always do?" asked Jack. "Or can we be up a little later?"

"Well-ll," said Mother, "I think——"

"Well," said Father, "let's put it this way. Go to bed in time to get eleven hours of sleep. You need that much sleep every night."

"Whee-ee!" sang Jack after Mother and Father had left. "We don't have to go to bed so early! We can be up later. Father said so!"

But Sue was not saying anything. She was busy thinking.

At last she said, "We get up at seven o'clock every morning, don't we, Jack?"

"Yes," said Jack. "Why?"

"Well, then," said Sue, "if we are to get eleven hours of sleep, we must go to bed right now. It's eight o'clock."

"Right now?" cried Jack. "Why, that is the time we always go to bed!"

"I know," laughed Sue. "Father didn't say we could be up later. He just used a new way to say 'Go to bed when you always go!'"

Not Sleepy

Bump, bump went Jack's shoes as he and Sue started upstairs to bed.

"Sh-h!" said Sue. "You will wake Tommy."

"Sh-h! So will you," said Jack.

Then they went on without talking.

Just as they went by Tommy's door, something came flying out at them.

"Oh!" cried Sue. "What is that?"

"It's Tim!" cried Jack. "It's Tommy's big old bunny rabbit. But how did it get out here?"

"We can soon find out," Sue said. So she and Jack went running into Tommy's room and put on the light.

There was Tommy, laughing at them!

"Boo-oo!" he said. "Boo-oo!"

"Oh, Tommy, you have been in bed for hours," said Sue. "You should be sleeping!"

"Tommy!" Jack said. "Go to sleep."

"No," said Tommy. "Not sleepy."

"Oh, dear!" thought Jack. "Tommy needs even more than eleven hours of sleep, and he isn't getting it."

Then he thought of something to do.

"Tommy," he said, "I don't think you know how to sleep. I really don't."

"Yes, I do," said Tommy. "Yes, I do."

"You will have to show me," Jack said.

So Tommy pretended to be sleeping.

And Jack waited and waited.

At last he said, "Tommy! Oh, Tommy!"

But Tommy didn't say anything.

"Oh, ho, Tommy!" thought Jack. "Who said you were not sleepy?"

A Busy Mother and Father

What Day Is It?

Bang, bang, bang went something downstairs.

"My!" thought Mother. "If I didn't know better, I would think someone was getting breakfast."

Bang, bang, bang went something downstairs again.

"What can that be?" thought Mother. "If I didn't know better, I would think someone was working downstairs. But it is too early for anyone in this house to be up."

"Jim," said Mother, "do you——"

But just then she saw that Father was not in his bed.

"Hm-m!" she thought. "Jim must be the one I hear downstairs. But what can he be doing so early?"

So she put on her housecoat and went down to see.

And there she saw Father and Jack and Sue and Tommy.

But they didn't see her. They were too busy—much too busy.

"My, but it is a lot of work to get breakfast," Sue was saying.

"Just think!" said Jack. "Mother does this every day, but it took all four of us to do it this morning."

"Now we know how busy Mother is," said Father.

"But she won't be busy today," Jack said. "We won't let her do any work."

"No, we won't," said Father. "Go and wake her now, Jack. Everything is ready, and won't she be surprised to see this good breakfast!"

Just then Mother said, "Here I am. And I am surprised! I think that I must be dreaming."

"Come and eat your fine breakfast," said Father. "Then you will know that you are not dreaming, Sally."

"But why didn't you tell me you wanted an early breakfast?" asked Mother. "I would have made it for you."

"Oh, no," said Jack. "Not today! We don't want you to do any work today."

"Well," said Mother, "I don't know what this is all about, but it is going to be a good day for me. A very good day!"

"It is a very good day," Father said. "The best day in the year."

"Yes," cried the children. "It is MOTHER'S DAY!"

Something for Mother

"We have something for you, Mother," said Jack. "Something for Mother's Day."

"Pictures," said Tommy. "Pictures for you."

"You see," Sue said, "we have been thinking that you have lots of work to do. And we are all going to help you more. Not just on Mother's Day but every day. Our pictures show how we will help."

"They show how I have been working the last week or so, too," laughed Father. "The children asked me to take pictures of them. And they made me work until I got just what they wanted."

Then Mother looked at the pictures, and this is what she saw.

My clothes won't be
On the floor.
Not any more!
No, not any more!
You won't have to say
"Tommy, put your toys away."
Every night
Here I'll be
Even without
Your telling me.
Arf! Arf! Arf!
Here is good news.
I will stop
Eating shoes.

A Safe House

"Do you know what it says here?" asked Father. "It says that many people get hurt right in their own homes!"

"In their own homes?" said Jack. "I thought people were safe when they were at home."

"Only if their homes are safe and they are careful," said Father. "Look at these pictures of how people get hurt at home."

So everyone came and looked at the pictures.

Here are some of the things that the pictures showed.

When they had looked at the pictures, Father said, "I guess we should look to see how safe our own house is."

"I'll look," said Sue. "You are busy reading, Father."

"I am not too busy to stop and see if our house is safe," said Father. "Come on! We will all look."

"Uh-oh!" said Sue. "Our stairs are not very safe. Someone might fall on these books and get hurt."

"Oh, dear!" cried Jack. "I won't put my books there any more."

Then the family went on looking. And everywhere they looked Sue told them what she thought they should do.

She thought Father should put something on this door. Something so that Tommy could not open it.

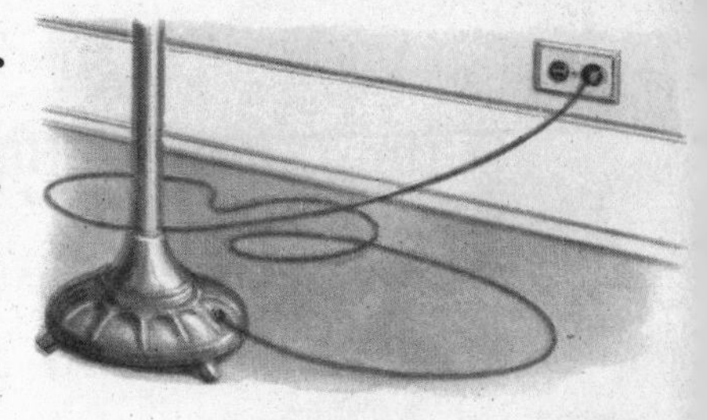

She thought Mother should push this back so that no one could fall over it.

She thought Tommy should keep this out of the doorway so that people would not fall over it.

At last they went into Sue's room.

"Let's look in here where you keep your clothes, Sue," said her mother. "I was thinking last week that this is not a very safe place."

"Oh, everything in this room is safe enough," said Sue. "I always keep things where I won't fall on them."

Then Sue opened a door.

Bump, bump! Bang, bang!

Down came some things on Sue.

Down, down on her head!

"Oh, my!" she cried. "I am not as careful as I thought I was.

I don't fall on things in my room. But things fall on me!"

Off to See the Doctor

"Hm-m!" said Father. "That was a good dinner, Sally.

And now I have a new book to read. My, but it is good to be home after a busy day!"

"Dear me!" said Mother. "I don't think you will have time to read that book. There is something we should do."

And then she told Father about a sign that was on some houses in the town.

A yellow sign that looked like this.

"Our children didn't go in any of these houses, did they?" asked Father.

"Oh, no!" Mother said. "They know better than that.

But they were very little when they were last vaccinated for smallpox, and I think they should be vaccinated again. Doctor Black says he will do it if we come to see him at seven o'clock."

A little later the Foster family was on the way to see the doctor.

"We are not sick," said Jack. "I don't see why we need to see a doctor."

"Sometimes a doctor can keep us from getting sick," said Father.

"Will it hurt when Doctor Black vaccinates us?" Sue asked.

"Maybe," said Mother. "But not much."

When they got to Doctor Black's, a nurse met them at the door.

"How do you do," she said. "What can we do for you?"

"I am Mr. Foster," said Father, "and this is my family. The doctor knows why we are here. He is going to vaccinate the children."

"That won't take long," the nurse said.

So she got the children ready to be vaccinated. Then she called the doctor.

"Hello, there," said Doctor Black. "I'll have you vaccinated before you know it. Come on, Sue. You first."

"Ow!" said Sue. "Maybe it will hurt."

Then the doctor put a little needle in her arm. In and out! He did that to Jack's arm and to Tommy's.

"There," he said. "Did that hurt?"

"Not much," Sue said. "But do hurry and vaccinate us so it will be over with."

"Oh, ho!" laughed Doctor Black. "You ARE vaccinated, all three of you."

"Well, what do you know about that?" laughed Sue. "We were vaccinated, and we didn't know it!"

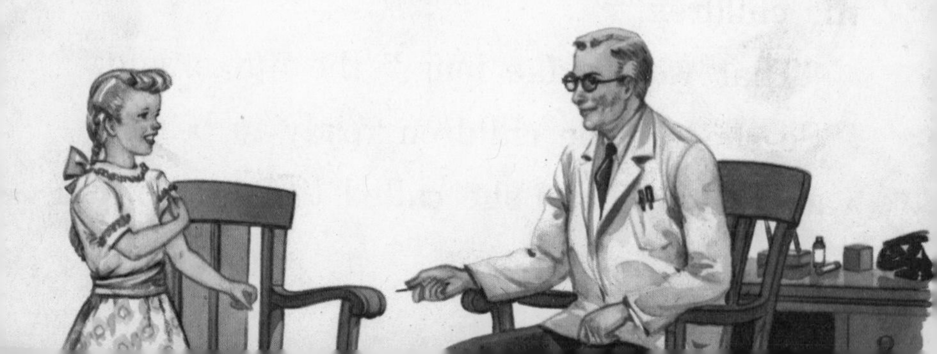

I Dare You!

"Hi, Sam!" called Jack. "Look at me! Don't you wish you could get up here, too?"

"Oh," said Sam, "I could get up there if I wanted to. But I dare you to jump down from there. I dare you!"

"Maybe I will jump, and maybe I won't," called Jack. "I may even fly down!"

"I dare you, I dare you, I dare you," Sam sang over and over. "I dare you to jump down from there."

"I could jump if I wanted to," Jack called. But he thought, "If I jump, I may get hurt. If I don't jump, Sam will think I can't take a dare. Oh, dear! I don't know what to do."

Just then who should come walking along but Miss Williams. When she looked up and saw Jack, she called, "Jack Foster! Come down from there. Come right down before you get hurt!"

"Whew!" thought Jack to himself. "I'll be glad to come down. And now I won't have to jump. Miss Williams came along just in time!"

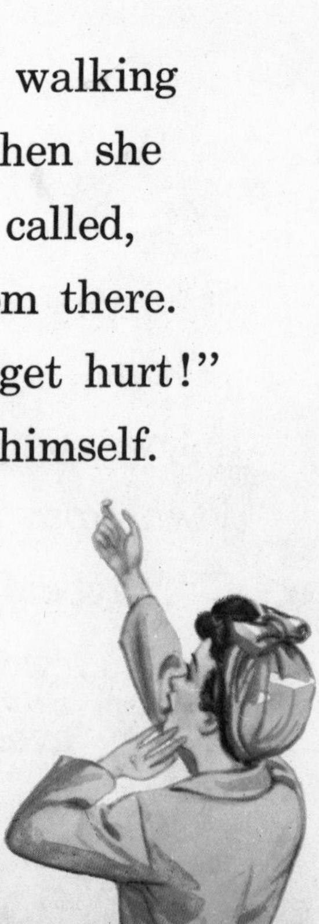

"Jack, Jack!" said Miss Williams after he had come down. "You were not really going to jump from there, were you?"

"Well," said Jack, "I was thinking about it. Sam dared me, and you have to take a dare, don't you?"

"Not a foolish dare to do something that isn't safe," Miss Williams said.

"And you, Sam," she went on, "you should not make foolish dares like that. Think how you would feel if Jack had jumped and been hurt!"

"Look!" said Jack, as Miss Williams went on down the street. "Look at me now, Sam."

"Oh, ho!" laughed Sam. "I dare you to go home looking like that. I dare you!"

"That is a safe enough dare," laughed Jack. "Just for the fun of it, I'll take that dare." And he did.

Which Were Foolish?

Which pictures show children who took dares that were foolish ones?

Why were the dares foolish?

A Letter from School

Splash, splash, splash went the rain on the windows.

Oo-oo, oo-oo-oo went the wind!

"My, but this is a cold, windy night," said Mother. "Summer will soon be here, but you really would not think so."

"This is a good night to be at home," said Father. "A good night to read my new book."

"Dear me!" Mother said. "Dear me, Jim! I don't think you are ever going to get that book read. This is the night we are to go to the school.

Don't you know? This is the night Miss Williams asked all the mothers and fathers to come."

Then Mother showed him the letter that had come from Miss Williams.

"Well, then," said Father, "I guess I'll go upstairs and get ready."

"Why are you going to school?" asked Jack. "What are you going to do there?"

"Sometimes we find out how you are getting along," said his mother. "And sometimes we just talk things over with Miss Williams."

"But this time we are going to make some plans," Father said. "Some plans for you."

"Look, Sue," said Jack when Mother and Father had gone to get ready. "Mother left that letter here. Let's read it and see why Miss Williams asked them to come to school."

"Oh, no!" Sue said. "Mother and Father don't read OUR letters. Not until we tell them they can. So we should not read their letters. Not until they tell us to."

"Well-ll," said Jack, "I won't read it. But I wish I could."

"I'll tell you what we can do," said Sue. "We can guess what that letter says. Then we can wait and see if we were right."

So that is what they did.

And that is what you can do, too.

A Surprise for the Children

"Summer will be here very soon," Miss Williams was saying.

"And this year the school is being all fixed over. People are working in the school yard, and the boys and girls can't play there.

That means the children won't have a good, safe place to play this summer. Even now they are playing in the street and in other places that are not safe."

"Why don't we make a playground for the children?" asked Mrs. Dick. "People do that in other towns. I don't see why we can't do it here."

"I own a big lot," said Mr. Robins, "and I will be glad to help make it into a playground."

"We will help," said Mr. and Mrs. Bird.

"And so will we," said the other mothers and fathers.

"Fine!" Miss Williams said. "We can start right now if you want to. We can use the school workshop to make some of the things we will need."

So they made some plans and then went to the workshop. They worked two hours that night. And some of them came back and worked night after night.

"I think we will soon have everything ready," said Mr. Dick, as he was painting some playthings one night.

"Oh, yes!" Mrs. Robins said. "I think everything will be ready by Saturday."

"My, but won't all the children be surprised!" laughed Mrs. Bird.

"I'll tell you what," said Mr. Gray. "We fathers will get everything ready by four o'clock next Saturday. And you mothers can come to the playground then with the children."

So that is what they did.

"Oh!" cried the children when they saw the new playground. "This is just what we wanted!"

"Look!" cried Jack. "A merry-go-round, a seesaw, and a place for our boats! Now we know what Miss Williams said in her letter. She told you we needed a playground."

"But we don't know how you found time to make all these things," said Sue.

"Well," said Mother, "you needed a good, safe place to play. So we made it for you. We can always find time for things like that."

Jack's Birthday Again

A Funny Surprise

"Just three more days," sang Jack. "Three more days until my birthday!"

"Another birthday?" Father said. "Soon you will be an old man, Jack."

"But you are not too old for a party, are you?" laughed Mother.

"I should say not," said Jack. "May I have a party, Mother? An outdoor one like the party I had last year?"

"Why, yes," Mother said. "If you will help me plan it. Three days won't give us much time, you know."

"We will all help," said Sue.

And they all did.

On the day of the party the children had lunch out in the back yard.

They had soup, sandwiches, fruit, cookies, nuts, and candy corn—all they could eat.

After lunch they started to play some games.

But Jill said, "Whew! I don't think I can play just now. I ate too much!"

"Well, then," said Jack, "maybe we should rest now and play later."

So they all sat down.

"Oh, ho!" said Jill, as they sat there. "I wish we could see the funny stunt you and Sue and Tommy did last year, Jack—the funny cowboy stunt."

"Do it for us again," said Don.

"Oh, yes!" cried Jill. "Please do."

"All right," Jack said. "If Mother can find our cowboy clothes, we will."

Then Jack and Sue and Tommy went inside. Soon they came out again in last year's cowboy clothes.

The others took a look at the cowboys, and then they began to laugh.

"What little clothes!" laughed Jill.

"What big cowboys!" laughed Don.

"You don't have to do the stunt with lassos," said Jill. "You are funny just as you are."

Then everyone laughed again.

"What is so funny?" asked Father, who was just coming home from work.

"Look at our cowboy clothes," said Jack. "They got too little for us."

"Oh, no!" laughed Father. "I think you got too big for them. And now I want you to stand right there until I can take your picture.

I think this will be the best of all your birthday pictures."

What Makes Us Grow?

A week later the picture that Father took was ready for the family to see.

After they had all laughed about it, Father showed them another picture.

"Oh!" said Jack. "That is how we looked last year, and this is how we look this year. Now I wish we could see how we will look next year."

"If we keep growing, we may be as big as Daddy," laughed Sue.

"I want to keep on growing," said Jack. "And I know what to do to grow big and strong and healthy."

"So do I," said Sue.

"So do I," said Tommy.

And so do you, don't you?

TO THE TEACHER

Five in the Family is the fourth Health and Personal Development book of the Curriculum Foundation Program. The important concepts of health, safety, and personal development introduced in this book are listed on pages 188-192.

All words in **Five in the Family,** except the 134 listed below, are words used in the preceding books of this series — **Happy Days, Good Times,** and **Three Friends.** For children who have completed The Basic Reading Series through **More Friends and Neighbors** (2^2), only the 47 words printed in boldface type in the list below will be new.

VOCABULARY LIST

UNIT I
6 picture
Tommy
7 —
8 grows
stunt
until
9 box
more
10 **soup**
sandwiches
11 rest
much
should
12 right
even
13 own
got
14 starts
15 wait
cried
16 **lasso**
17 **Daddy**
I'll
18 —

UNIT II
19 neighbors
20 —
21 keep
22 mouse
plant
best
23 left
won't
really
24 their
25 if
26 about
27 **weighs**
than
been
28 **pounds**
29 enough
30 **plan**
would
31 **throws**
hand
32 **Foster**
33 use
whew
whiz
34 lots
35 show
careful
36 stand
honk
37 sign
germs
spread
38 inside
before
mouth
39 —
40 —
41 clean
himself
42 these
paper
43 long
44 matter
45 sunlight
46 strong
healthy
47 Saturday
football
game
48 **eleven**
o'clock
49 only
window
50 —
51 off
52 —
53 might
54 —
55 people
fruit
56 **feel**
better
57 —
58 means
dry
59 shoes
gave
60 **clay**

61 —
62 —

UNIT III

63 —
64 **beauty**
shop
65 fix
hair
66 —
67 —
68 week
towels
69 straight
70 fall
71 —
72 —
73 **vegetables**
bones
74 —
75 —
76 —
77 —
78 by
79 —
80 **muscles**
81 coat
82 —
83 **thermometer**
84 —
85 stairs
radio
86 —
87 hear
88 **program**
89 angry
chair
90 **puppet**
91 —
92 —
93 eyes
94 **nurse**
95 place
drink
96 told
97 —
98 —
99 —
100 ever
101 —
102 most
103 —
104 —

UNIT IV

105 —
106 **dirty**
107 —
108 —
109 —
110 —
111 **custard**
112 **glass**
113 —
114 —
115 —
116 —
117 —
118 —
119 —
120 **fit**
121 —
122 machine
123 —
124 —
125 —
126 care
127 —
128 —
129 —
130 —
131 **safe**
132 —
133 —
134 —
135 —
136 **dentist**
137 —
138 —
139 —
140 —
141 —
142 **needles**
143 gone
144 **doctor**
145 —
146 **hours**
147 **seven**
eight
148 —
149 —
150 —

UNIT V

151 —
152 —
153 —
154 —
155 —
156 —
157 —
158 —
159 —
160 —
161 —
162 —
163 —
164 **vaccinate**
smallpox
165 —
166 arm
167 **dare**
168 —
169 **foolish**
170 —
171 —
172 letter
summer
173 —
174 —
175 —
176 playground
177 —
178 —

UNIT VI

179 —
180 —
181 —
182 —
183 —
184 —

Important Concepts Introduced in *Five in the Family*

Five in the Family is an account of one year with the Fosters, a typical family with three lively children, aged two, eight, and ten. The stories in this book center around the day-by-day experiences of the family members, their relationships with each other and with friends and neighbors. A special attempt is made to make the family members come alive as individuals—to portray their individual problems and to indicate how each one is learning to cope with his particular problems relating to health, safety, and personal adjustment.

The list below and on succeeding pages shows the important concepts of health, safety, and personal adjustment which may be developed from the stories in *Five in the Family*. These concepts, which are inherent in the lively, interesting stories, are not explained didactically but may be brought out under teacher guidance in informal discussions concerning the activities of the story characters. In this way children are helped to form their own standards and habits of self-discipline. Moreover, the teacher, noting children's reactions to the various story incidents, will frequently gain insight into emotional and personal problems requiring parent-teacher coöperation. In dealing with problems of this kind, suggestions in the book *Parents and Children Go to School*[1] by Dorothy Baruch will be helpful to both teachers and parents.

Five in the Family reviews the important concepts developed in the two preceding books of the series, *Good Times* and *Three Friends*. It also extends the concepts previously touched upon and introduces others in keeping with the child's increasing maturity.

UNIT ONE — A Birthday in the Family

Happy Birthday (pages 6-9)

Opening story to introduce the Foster family: Jack, age 8; Tommy, age 2; Sue, age 10; Mother and Father.

Leads for discussing various ways families record the growth of children from year to year.

Fun at the Party (pages 10-13)

HEALTH: Desirability of a brief rest period after eating and before engaging in strenuous activity.

Consideration of what constitutes a good, healthful lunch.

The Three Stunts (pages 14-16)

HEALTH: Value of playing outdoors whenever possible.

PERSONAL DEVELOPMENT: A little ingenuity can provide a lot of fun—elaborate equipment is not always necessary.

Father Takes a Picture (pages 17-18)

HEALTH: Growth from year to year is often best recorded through family snapshots and moving pictures. Leads for stimulating an exhibit of children's records of their own growth.

[1]Scott, Foresman and Company, 1939.

UNIT TWO — Jack and the New Neighbors

Good-by to Bill and Ellen (pages 20-23)

PERSONAL DEVELOPMENT: Giving gifts is fun if you really *want* to give them. Leads for discussing acts of friendliness that make social relationships more pleasant.

The New Neighbors (pages 24-26)

PERSONAL DEVELOPMENT: Interest in other people and friendly acceptance of new children is a sign of good adjustment.

Something New for the Family (pages 27-29) and *work page 30*

HEALTH: Desirability of keeping weight records *if* they are not used as "absolute" measures of healthy development.

PERSONAL DEVELOPMENT: Awareness that there is no *exact* weight for any child at any given age—too much stress should not be placed on gaining weight as children may become anxious when they don't make anticipated gains.

The New Boy (pages 31-34)

HEALTH: Need for outdoor play after school when weather permits.

PERSONAL DEVELOPMENT: Left-handedness need not be a handicap—at times it has distinct advantages! Children should use whichever hand is the more natural for them.

New friends can be as much fun as old ones—new children in a school or neighborhood want and need to be "taken in" and made a part of a group.

A Busy Street (pages 35-36)

SAFETY: Safety precautions to observe in crossing streets.

A Morning at School (pages 37-40)

HEALTH: Understanding of some of the ways by which diseases are spread.

Jack's Plan (pages 41-42)

HEALTH: Children can learn to assume responsibility for washing hands before eating or handling food.

PERSONAL DEVELOPMENT: Desirability of *doing something* about health ideas gained at school.

The Plant and the Mouse (pages 43-46)

HEALTH: All living things need plenty of food, water, and sunshine.

PERSONAL ADJUSTMENT: Responsibility (at least partial) of children for taking care of pets, plants, etc., in the home.

Ready or Not? (pages 47-50)

HEALTH: Desirable morning routine—need for making this routine a habit. Good eating habits—eating slowly and chewing food well.

PERSONAL ADJUSTMENT: Being ready at an appointed time is a courteous act—and children can gradually be led to appreciate this.

Off to the Football Game (pages 51-53)

SAFETY: Importance of observing traffic lights, waiting for approaching trains, and keeping to the left when walking on the road.

The Football Game (pages 54-56)

HEALTH: Candy eaten between meals dulls the appetite. Leads for discussing healthful between-meal snacks; e.g., milk, sandwiches, fruit.

One Rainy Day (pages 57-59)

HEALTH: Desirability of removing wet clothes as soon as possible. Need for rubbers and boots in wet weather—especially when walking in puddles!

Playing with Clay (pages 60-62)

PERSONAL DEVELOPMENT: Sometimes it's well to find your own way of doing things. Also, there are times when you have to assert yourself—especially if someone in the group is officious.

UNIT THREE — Sue and Her Friends

A Beauty Shop at Home (pages 64-68)

HEALTH: Proper care of hair, need for own comb and brush, etc.

PERSONAL DEVELOPMENT: Dramatizing things that can't actually be done is fun—and good mental hygiene, too.

Father's Pictures (pages 69-71) and *work page 72*

HEALTH: Effect of good posture on general appearance.

Leads for emphasizing influence on posture of good food, rest, and general good health. All these factors contribute to strong, straight bodies.

Vegetable Surprises (pages 73-77)

HEALTH: Function of vegetables in making strong bones and healthy teeth.

PERSONAL DEVELOPMENT: Obligation of guests to eat what is served. Opening for discussing the idea that sometimes food dislikes are fancied and that new ways of cooking vegetables make them unexpectedly palatable.

Sue's Book about Foods (pages 78-80)

HEALTH: Different foods do different things for us: some build strong bones and teeth, some build muscles, some keep us well and help us grow.

Sue Always Knows (pages 81-85) and *work page 86*

HEALTH: Need for adapting clothing to weather conditions; ways of forecasting what the weather will be; proper room temperature for a house in winter; use of the thermometer, etc.

Sue and the Radio (pages 87-89)

HEALTH: Desirability of resting a little after eating.

PERSONAL DEVELOPMENT: Sometimes an individual's personal desires must give way to the desires of the group.

Sue's Cold (pages 90-95) and **How Do We Get Colds?** (pages 96-97)

HEALTH: Care of colds; inadvisability of trying to "keep going" when one has a cold; ways in which colds are spread; ways in which colds may be started. Review of desirable morning routine.

PERSONAL DEVELOPMENT: Responsibility of children for telling parents when they are not feeling well—and for staying home when ill.

A Plan for Sue (pages 98-101) and **Who Had the Most Fun?** (pages 102-104)

HEALTH: One way of preventing spread of colds is to keep away from others when suffering from a cold.

PERSONAL DEVELOPMENT: It's fun to do things for others!

UNIT FOUR — Fun with Tommy

Who Did It? (pages 106-110)

HEALTH: Review of need for washing before eating; desirability of each individual having and using his own towel and washcloth.

PERSONAL DEVELOPMENT: Little children can't be judged by their acts alone; their motives must be considered. Often what seems like mischief is only a genuine desire to help or to be independent.

A Plan That Worked Too Well (pages 111-114) and *work page 115*

HEALTH: Milk and eggs are essential to health and growth; most people need three to four glasses of milk a day; dishes made from milk are worth-while variations in the daily diet and one means of getting daily milk requirements.

PERSONAL DEVELOPMENT: Older children may find satisfaction at times in setting behavior patterns that are worthy ones for younger children to emulate.

Tommy Reads a Story (pages 116-119)

HEALTH: Need for good light when reading; knowledge of what constitutes a good reading light. Leads for discussing other ways to safeguard the eyes: proper distance to hold book from eyes, periodic eye examinations, etc.

Shoes That Fit (pages 120-124)

HEALTH: Importance of well-fitting shoes; responsibility of children for helping judge how well their shoes fit; interpretation of "feet pictures"; desirability of keeping shoes shined.

What Is the Matter with Sue? (pages 125-128)

PERSONAL DEVELOPMENT: Feelings of jealousy are not unique in any individual—but a frank discussion of such feelings is better than pouting; parents may not like annoying actions, but their love for the "wrongdoer" is not affected; family needs must be cared for as they arise, and not everyone can have new clothes at the same time.

Tommy Goes to a Fire (pages 129-132) and **What to Do about Fires** (pages 133-135)

SAFETY: Dangers of playing with fire; ways of giving a fire alarm; understanding of what to do if one's clothing catches on fire.

Tommy Goes to the Dentist (pages 136-139) and *work pages 140-141*

HEALTH: Importance of a wholesome attitude toward visits to the dentist; proper care of the teeth; leads for discussing the part vegetables, fruit, and milk play in helping make strong, healthy teeth.

Tommy and the Needles (pages 142-145)

SAFETY: Importance of keeping pins, needles, and other small objects out of the reach of little children.

PERSONAL DEVELOPMENT: Need for keeping calm and getting the facts in a "crisis."

Bedtime (pages 146-147) and **Not Sleepy** (pages 148-150)

HEALTH: Children of eight to ten years need to average approximately eleven hours of sleep each night, and younger children require even more sleep, although there are individual differences in sleep requirements; regular bedtime habits are desirable; leads for discussing value of getting enough sleep each night.

UNIT FIVE — A Busy Mother and Father

What Day Is It? (pages 152-155)

HEALTH: Leads for discussing what constitutes a good breakfast.

PERSONAL DEVELOPMENT: Helping Mother is one of the best ways of honoring her on Mother's Day, birthdays, and other special occasions.

Something for Mother (pages 156-157)

HEALTH: Frequent bathing is essential to healthful living.

PERSONAL DEVELOPMENT: Children in the home should assume some responsibility for picking up toys, hanging up clothes, etc.

A Safe House (pages 158-162)

SAFETY: Common causes of accidents in the home; responsibility of family members in helping avoid such accidents.

Off to See the Doctor (pages 163-166)

HEALTH: The quarantine sign—what it means, how it helps us; leads for discussing doctor's work and for creating wholesome attitudes toward doctors.

PERSONAL DEVELOPMENT: Looking after a family's needs often calls for sacrifice on the part of parents—the things they want to do must frequently be put aside for the things they feel they must do.

I Dare You! (pages 167-170) and *work page 171*

SAFETY: Safe places versus unsafe places to play.

PERSONAL DEVELOPMENT: Foolish dares should not be made—and should not be taken! Harmless dares made just for fun are another matter.

A Letter from School (pages 172-174)

PERSONAL DEVELOPMENT: Leads for discussing the idea that it is quite common for parents and teachers to meet and talk over mutual problems—and very desirable, too.

Reading other people's mail is "no fair" unless you are asked to do so.

A Surprise for the Children (pages 175-178)

SAFETY: Values of having and using playgrounds; leads for considering safety precautions to be used with typical playground equipment.

PERSONAL DEVELOPMENT: Parents and teachers frequently are good friends who work together for the good of the children.

UNIT SIX — Jack's Birthday Again

A Funny Surprise (pages 180-183)

HEALTH: Review of the desirability of resting a little after eating and before engaging in strenuous activity; development of the concept of growth—one year *does* make a difference, and the evidence of that is not hard to find!

What Makes Us Grow? (pages 184-185)

HEALTH: Provision for a review of all the factors that help boys and girls grow strong and keep healthy: adequate sleep, good nutrition, plenty of fresh air and sunshine, cleanliness, regularity of habits, etc.

Leads for discussing evidences of how children themselves have grown in the past semester or year; e.g., weight and height increases, change in size of shoes, stockings, coats, and the like.

7 8 9 10 11 12 13 14 15 16 17 18 19 20 21 22 23 24 25 55 54 53 52 51 50